The

Chartered psycho...
illustrator Nick H... ...p
to create a playful and uplifting guide
to positive thinking. Sam has spent many
years helping people take positive action
in their lives by making self-help strategies
engaging, practical and easy to use.

Read the psychologist's top tips and integrate
them into your motivated life.

Enjoy the journey!

To:

With positive thoughts from:

Energy Boost

Our energy levels have a significant impact on our motivation levels.

A natural way to keep your energy levels and consequent motivation levels high is to exercise regularly.

Exercise will build up your physical endurance and strengthen your drive to be productive.

Create a weekly plan to help make exercise a healthy routine and protect against low motivation.

Magical Momentum

Motivation levels suffer when our goals seem too large to achieve. When you set a goal, identify several simple actions that you can accomplish quickly to start making immediate progress.

The 17th century scientist Isaac Newton noted that "An object at rest stays at rest and an object in motion stays in motion". Take action, because if you start moving towards your goal it may become harder to stop than to keep going!

The Magic Of Music

Listening to music is a good way to generate motivation.

Create a compilation of motivational songs to put on CD or your Ipod.

Listening to music before sleep, during work (when appropriate) and whilst travelling can become a powerful tool to be positive when your motivation is tested.

Push Outside
The Comfort Zone

To keep your motivation high, push outside the comfort zone.

As a rule of thumb, commit to doing one difficult thing every day.

Being adventurous day-to-day will inject zest into your life and keep you hungry and motivated for more.

Super Stretching

Stretching improves the circulation of blood and helps the delivery of energy throughout the body. When you feel your motivation levels dipping take a few minutes to stretch your arms, back, legs and neck. Hold your stretch for 5 seconds, take a deep breath through your nose and release the stretch position as you breathe out through your mouth. Repeat this several times until your mind and body feel focused and relaxed.

Great Goal-Setting

Goal setting is a highly effective tool for injecting focus and direction into your life.

When you are setting a long-term goal, break it down into small steps that will build up to the long-term target. Produce a flow chart – a roadmap to success.

Keep your roadmap visible in your working space to maintain strong and purposeful motivation.

Positive Self-Talk

Feed your mind with a positive voice. Talk to yourself at key times, internally and out loud, using words of encouragement.

Repeated regularly, phrases such as "I have the motivation to succeed" and "I feel good and up for the challenge" will strengthen your motivation.

The benefits of this strategy will be even more enhanced if you create your own positive phrases.

Successful Activities

When you have pressing deadlines and need to be successful quickly, it is easy to fool yourself that you can work for lengthy periods of time without a break.

It is, however, more effective to work in short but regular bursts of activity.

It will make your goals seem more achievable and it will dramatically boost productivity and your overall motivation.

Motivation Buddies

Social pressure is an effective way to ensure that you stick to your good intentions.

This is particularly effective in the context of sticking to an exercise regime.

Tell friends and family whenever you set goals. This will create a healthy pressure and added motivation to stay on track.

Values

The true measure of success is to live your life according to your values - core principles such as honesty, creativity, learning and caring for your family.

If you set goals that are not aligned with your values, your motivation will suffer. Make a list of your life values and ensure that your goals fall in line with them before venturing forwards.

End Goals Can Work Against You

When you become too attached to outcomes, you lose focus on the actions that you need to take in order to achieve them.

You can't control outcomes but you can control your actions. If your mind is overly focused on the end product, the motivation to make it happen will be damaged. Take time to break your objectives down into a list of key actions and focus only on completing them. Positive outcomes will then follow.

Magic Water

Your day-to-day energy levels have a big impact on your motivation. One way to keep energy levels flying high is to drink plenty of water. It is medically proven that even a small reduction in water intake can have a negative impact on energy levels. The secret to drinking regularly is to make water easily accessible. If you carry a sports bottle with you when appropriate, the visual reminder of the bottle will encourage regular drinking.

A Greater Cause

You are much more likely to find the motivation to achieve your goals if there is an external incentive greater than yourself driving them. For example individuals who run marathons to raise money for charity find the time and energy to train hard for their event because of their greater mission. So if, for example, you have the goal of writing a novel, you should see it as an opportunity to create an engaging and enjoyable read for other people. Inspiration and motivation will come more easily when your goals are focused on the needs of other people rather than just your own.

Great Minds Think Alike

People who have made achievements personally and professionally have similar mindsets.

They have in common the key characteristics of tenacity, determination, and discipline.

Read autobiographies of individuals who you admire to gain insight into their behaviour and to understand the psychology that has driven them to be successful.

Document the mental strategies that would add value your own mindset and use this to keep your motivation high.

The Power Of
Written Intentions

When you write down your goals you increase the likelihood that you will act upon them.

It creates a personal contract and gives you a positive nudge whenever motivation is proving hard to find. Make time to write down your daily intentions and tick them off as you complete them. This will also generate a sense of progression and momentum that will help to keep motivation levels high.

Quiet Time

It is unrealistic to think that you can be productive all of the time. If you try to do too much your efforts will end up working against you. In the busy lives we lead it is advisable to find time to detach and switch off for short periods. Finding the time to quieten the mind and be still will recharge your batteries and strengthen your overall motivation. By sitting quietly on your own for a while, you will create the opportunity to return to your work with a fresh and clear perspective. Start by taking 10 minutes out each day to nourish your mind and body with peace and quiet. Your overall motivation will benefit.

The Win List

Whenever you make achievements in your life, document them. Start compiling a win list in your journal. Take 5 minutes every week to update your list and visualise yourself as you achieved each of your successes.

This will help the mind and body stay motivated to keep on achieving!

Ignite The Engine

The biggest predictor of your behaviour is your state of mind. Enjoyment is a potent reward and it will work on its own as an effective motivator.

Before starting an important task check that you are in a resourceful state. If you are not, just close your eyes for a few seconds and think about something that makes you feel good. Then you will be ready to begin.

Super Surroundings

Having a supportive environment
will keep motivation high.

Always surround yourself
with objects of comfort
while you are working.

A comfortable chair to sit in,
a clear and well organised working
space, photos of loved ones and easy
access to all the tools you will need
will keep you in a flow state
with high motivation.

Strike While
The Iron Is Hot!

Our energy levels naturally ebb and flow during the day.

Make a note of those times during the day when you feel most energised and reserve them for the most challenging tasks.

When your energy levels naturally dip you will be left with the tasks that can be completed more easily.

Directing your focus onto the right tasks at the right time is important in maintaining your levels of motivation.

The Pocket Psychologist™
Other Titles in the Series

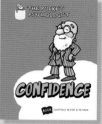

Published by Mindsport Ltd in 2012 - All rights reserved.
Printed in China

Mindsport Ltd
72 Prince Street, Bristol, BS1 4QD, United Kingdom
www.MyPositiveUniverse.com